STRENGTH

OPTIMISM

Sara Antill

PowerKiDS press™

New York

For Jeremy, with high hopes for the next 50 years…

Published in 2014 by The Rosen Publishing Group, Inc.
29 East 21st Street, New York, NY 10010

Copyright © 2014 by The Rosen Publishing Group, Inc.

First Edition

Editor: Jennifer Way
Book Design: Greg Tucker

Photo Credits: Cover Peathegee Inc/Blend Images/Getty Images; p. 4 Chip Somodevilla/ Getty Images; p. 5 Jonathan Gelber/Getty Images; p. 6 Ryan McVay/Lifesize/Getty Images; p. 7 ColorBlind Images/Blend Images/Getty Images; p. 8 Digital Vision/Thinkstock; p. 9 Jupiterimages/Creatas/Thinkstock; p. 10 George Gojkovich/Getty Images; p. 11 Jupiterimages/Pixland/Thinkstock; p. 13 Robin Marchant/FilmMagic/Getty Images; p. 14 Popperfoto/Getty Images; p. 15 Ken Chernus/Stone/Getty Images; p. 17 Creatista/ Shutterstock.com; p. 18 Tetra Images/Getty Images; p. 19 Jenkedco/Shutterstock.com; p. 20 Howard Sochurek/Time & Life Pictures/Getty Images; p. 21 Monkey Business Images/ Shutterstock.com.

Library of Congress Cataloging-in-Publication Data

Antill, Sara.
  Optimism / by Sara Antill. — 1st ed.
      p. cm. — (Character strength)
  Includes index.
  ISBN 978-1-4488-9682-0 (library binding) — ISBN 978-1-4488-9822-0 (pbk.) —
  ISBN 978-1-4488-9823-7 (6-pack)
  1. Optimism. 2. Success. I. Title.
  BF698.35.O57A58 2013
  149'.5—dc23
                          2012030177

Manufactured in the United States of America

CPSIA Compliance Information: Batch #S13PK2: For Further Information contact Rosen Publishing, New York, New York at 1-800-237-9932

Contents

Success and Attitude   4

What Is Optimism?   6

Expect the Best!   8

Focus on the Positive   10

He's an Optimist!   12

An Inner Resource   14

Encouraging Others   16

Growing Your Optimism   18

Finding a Balance   20

My Report Card: Optimism   22

Glossary   23

Index   24

Websites   24

SUCCESS AND ATTITUDE

Think of a successful person whom you have met or read about. It might be an inventor, an athlete, or even the president of the United States. What kind of **attitude** do you think that person has about life? Do you think he believes he can do great things? This attitude is called **optimism**. Optimism is a character strength that helps many people succeed.

Barack Obama (1961-)

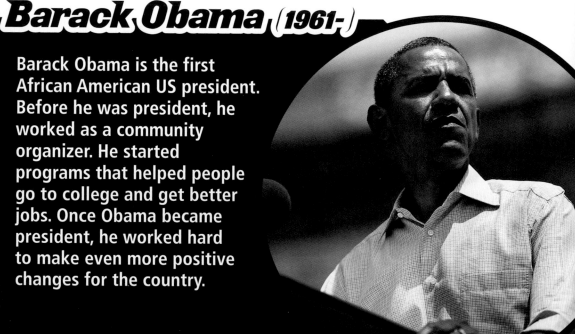

Barack Obama is the first African American US president. Before he was president, he worked as a community organizer. He started programs that helped people go to college and get better jobs. Once Obama became president, he worked hard to make even more positive changes for the country.

When you are feeling optimistic, you might walk with a little extra spring in your step!

When Barack Obama was running for president, he often used the words "Yes we can." He wanted people to believe that a better future was possible. Believing that things can get better is a big part of optimism!

WHAT IS OPTIMISM?

People with optimism are called optimists. They live with a positive outlook. People with **negative** attitudes are called **pessimists**. They expect the worst things to happen. People with optimism, though, expect the best possible results.

Optimistic people make the best of situations. Rain might not be your favorite weather, but you can enjoy splashing in the puddles!

Optimists wake up "on the right side of the bed." That means they start their day with a good attitude.

Have you ever done poorly on a test at school? A person with optimism does not focus on setbacks or failures. When you live with optimism, you expect the best and are willing to work hard to reach your goals. Many optimists visualize, or picture themselves, doing something well. They believe that doing this helps them improve and achieve the results they want.

EXPECT THE BEST!

When you live with optimism, you should expect the best from yourself! When you face a new challenge, believe that you can succeed. This means you have **confidence** in yourself. If people did not believe that they could be successful, they would never try new things. Go into new **situations** with an attitude of "I can" instead of "I cannot."

Learning to play an instrument is challenging. If you approach your lessons with optimism, you will feel confident that you can do it.

An optimistic person might be more likely to make healthy eating choices. He knows that his body deserves to be taken care of.

It is important to be optimistic about the success of others, too. When people know that you have confidence in them, they will likely try harder. When someone tries harder, he or she is even more likely to succeed!

FOCUS ON THE POSITIVE

It can be hard to control your feelings when something goes wrong. When you are having a bad day, it is natural to feel upset. However, looking at the positive side of things can help you feel better.

You can control your behavior, though. You can choose to focus on the positive.

Michael Oher (1986-)

Michael Oher plays in the National Football League (NFL) for the Baltimore Ravens. Oher spent much of his childhood in foster care. In high school, he discovered his love of football. Despite the hardships he went through, Oher believed that if he worked hard at football and at school, he could change his life.

If you are having a bad day, it can help to talk to someone who can cheer you up.

Michael Oher wrote in his memoir, *I Beat the Odds*, about how sports became an important positive part of his life. He also had positive **role models** who helped him focus on his goals. This helped him go from a homeless teenager to a professional football player.

HE'S AN OPTIMIST!

Michael J. Fox is a film and television actor. In 1998, he announced he had an illness called Parkinson's disease. Parkinson's disease makes it hard for people to control their body movements. Their bodies may shake, and they have trouble walking. Because of the disease, Fox was not able to do as much acting as he used to.

When some people find out they have serious diseases, they might get angry. Fox chose to look on the positive side, though. He started a foundation to help find a cure for Parkinson's disease. He calls himself an optimist and has said that he sees possibilities in everything.

ox.org

Fox started the Michael J. Fox Foundation in 2000.
This foundation raises awareness about Parkinson's
and helps fund research to cure the disease.

AN INNER RESOURCE

To succeed at something, you first have to try. If you are going to try, you must first believe there is a chance of success. In this way, optimism is an inner **resource** that helps you succeed.

People with optimism set goals and believe that it is possible to reach those goals.

Franklin Delano Roosevelt (1882-1945)

Franklin Delano Roosevelt became president of the United States during the **Great Depression**. Many people had lost their jobs. Families were struggling to survive. In an important speech, Roosevelt said, "The only thing we have to fear is fear itself." He wanted people to believe that although times were hard, things would get better.

Optimistic people believe they can make the world a better place. They might volunteer for causes, such as building housing for poor people.

Instead of focusing on what could go wrong, they focus on ways they can grow and become better. Franklin D. Roosevelt was president during the Great Depression and World War II. The optimism he expressed kept Americans **motivated** to work together during those difficult times.

When others around you are negative, it is easy to feel negative, too. When those around you are positive and optimistic, though, it is easier for you to feel optimistic. Encourage your friend. **Encouraging** optimism in others will help you show your optimism, too!

If you see that a friend is upset, let her know you are there to talk. Instead of focusing on the negative, though, talk about ways you can solve the problem together. Let her know that things will get better. If you have a friend who always looks on the bright side, cheer him on, too!

Everyone has the power to bring the people around them down or to encourage them to do their best. An optimistic person helps keep the other dancers in her class motivated.

GROWING YOUR OPTIMISM

It can be hard when someone points out your faults. For example, your teacher might give you a low grade or remind you to pay more attention in class. It is important not to get upset when this happens, though. People with optimism understand that seeing their mistakes can help them grow and do better next time.

Taking criticism from a teacher is never easy. An optimist will try to learn from his mistakes and feel motivated to improve.

Focusing on the positive can change both your outlook and the results you get. It makes a big difference to think of goals as what you intend to achieve rather than what you wish to achieve.

If you find yourself focusing on the negative side of things, do not feel bad. Remember that you can always control your behavior. When you are upset, think of the best possible way that something could turn out. Imagine the future. Then take action to make it happen!

FINDING A BALANCE

Optimism is one of the most important character strengths you can have. It can help you create positive goals and then reach them. Scientists have found that optimistic people even live longer than pessimistic people!

There are other strengths that can help you succeed, too. These include grit, self-control, curiosity, and zest, or enthusiasm. It is important to balance these strengths.

Martin Luther King Jr. (1929-1968)

Martin Luther King Jr. was a **civil rights** leader who worked to end segregation between whites and African Americans. In 1963, he gave a famous speech called the "I have a dream" speech. In it, he talked about his hopes for a better future. He believed that one day all races of people would be treated equally. His dream is getting ever closer to coming true.

Grit is a character strength that makes you want to work hard even if that work is tough. Your optimism tells you that your hard work will be worth it.

Someone with too much optimism or zest may start to believe that things will turn out for the best even if she does not try hard. Balancing your strengths will help you use them in the best way for success.

MY REPORT CARD:
OPTIMISM

On a separate piece of paper, take this test. How many of the following statements about optimism are true about you? Be honest! Do not be upset if you do not get a perfect score. Practice showing your optimism for a while, and then take the test again.

- ☐ I always look on the bright side.
- ☐ I respond well to criticism.
- ☐ I believe that things can always get better.
- ☐ I know if I try hard, I will get good results.
- ☐ I often think positive thoughts.
- ☐ I like to think about how I can get better at things.
- ☐ When I get frustrated or upset, I usually get over it quickly.
- ☐ I expect the best from others and myself.
- ☐ I encourage others to focus on the positive.
- ☐ I set goals and then try my best to reach them.

Glossary

attitude (A-tuh-tood) A person's outlook or position.

civil rights (SIH-vul RYTS) The rights that citizens have.

confidence (KON-fih-dents) A firm belief in something or someone.

encouraging (in-KUR-ij-ing) Giving hope, cheer, or certainty.

Great Depression (GRAYT dih-PREH-shun) A period of American history during the late 1920s and early 1930s. Banks and businesses lost money and there were few jobs.

motivated (MOH-tih-vayt-ed) Gave someone a reason to do something.

negative (NEH-guh-tiv) Looking at the bad side of things.

optimism (OP-tuh-mih-zum) A state in which one has the most favorable understanding of events or foresees the most favorable outcome.

pessimists (PEH-suh-mists) People who expect bad things to happen.

resource (REE-sawrs) A supply, source of energy, or useful thing.

role models (ROHL MAH-dulz) People who show others good behavior.

situations (sih-choo-AY-shunz) Problems or events.

Index

A
Americans, 14–15, 20

C
confidence, 8–9

F
future, 5, 19–20

G
Great Depression, 14–15

I
inventor, 4

J
jobs, 4, 14

K
kind, 4
King, Martin Luther, Jr., 20

L
life, 4, 10–11

O
Obama, Barack, 4–5
outlook, 6

P
person, 4–9, 12, 14, 18, 20
pessimists, 6
president, 4–5, 14–15
programs, 4

R
results, 6–7, 22
role models, 11

S
school, 7, 10
situations, 8

Websites

Due to the changing nature of Internet links, PowerKids Press has developed an online list of websites related to the subject of this book. This site is updated regularly. Please use this link to access the list: www.powerkidslinks.com/char/opti/